Six Advent Plays For Children

Doris Wells Miller

CSS Publishing Company, Inc., Lima, Ohio

For more information about CSS Publishing Company resources, visit our website at www.csspub.com or email us at custserv@csspub.com or call (800) 241-4056.

Cover Design by Barbara Spencer
ISBN-13: 978-0-7880-2407-8

PRINTED IN U.S.A.

This book is dedicated to the Cambridge Drive Community Church in Goleta, California. Our church is a small, family-oriented congregation that is truly intergenerational. Every child knows that their church family contains not only their immediate parents and siblings, but many loving grandmas and grandpas and children of all ages to play with and to learn how God loves them. Christian education for adults, as well as children, is very important to us.

Table Of Contents

Guidelines For Directors

1. **Program**
   a. Begin the process in September by selecting the program.
   b. Clear the date and time for presentation of the program with the church calendar. It should be a day that will not conflict with children going to visit relatives for the holiday or with public school activities.
   c. Consider the length of the production. When young children are involved, the program needs to be less than an hour in length. Sometimes half an hour is a good limit.

2. **Selection**
   a. Prepare the material. For a play, twice as many scripts are needed as you would think.
   b. Count the number and ages of the children available. Be sure to include children with special capabilities, talents, or needs.

3. **Planning**
   It is important to have the support of your teaching staff, church leaders, and the pastor.
   a. **Music:** Is there a youth choir? Are there soloists? Selections noted in the dramas are only suggestions and are found in most church hymnals. However, if there is music that is preferred and it fits into the theme, by all means, use it. Avoid presenting secular music.
   b. **Musicians:** Find a pianist or guitarist who will work with the children during their Sunday school hour or better yet, during the week. Give the musician a few months' advance notice.
   c. **Assistants: The director cannot do everything alone.** Enlist teachers, friends, parents, or someone in the church family to assist. The assistants will need to be at each rehearsal to help the children with their parts, plan and prepare sets, props, and lighting, and to give feedback.
   d. **Rehearsals:** Plan the days and times for the rehearsals and program. Clear this with the church calendar. A good time for dress rehearsal *(one rehearsal is enough for young children)* is the day before presentation. This also gives time for last minute mending and ironing of costumes.
   e. **Party:** We follow our program with a family Christmas party to which we invite the children, parents, families, and friends. We request, in advance, that parents bring a plate of goodies that evening. A committee (or the church) could provide punch and coffee. Plan on this party to be at the church or ask a church member to open his home and prepare a table to serve. Arrange for the singing of Christmas carols and an accompanist. Our church uses this occasion to distribute Christmas thank-you gifts to the pastor and staff.
   f. **Recording production:** Arrange for someone to make a recording that can be enjoyed for years. Many parents may want to purchase copies.

4. **Rehearsals**
   a. Request permission from the Sunday school superintendent or teachers, in early November, to gather all the grade school children in one place to read the play or program script. If it is a large group, this may be done in two sessions.
   b. Let the children know that they will be participating in a special Christmas program. Read the entire script to them once. On the second reading assign a different child to read each part. Then, at the start of each act; assign another set of children to do the same. **The director narrates** to give more control and direction. Following this reading, inform the children that a letter will be sent

home with them regarding the first rehearsal date and time. At that time they will be assigned their parts.

c. Prepare two letters to go home with the children the day of the play reading.

The first letter should read: "We are planning a special Christmas program on December ____ in the _____ room of the church. Your child will have an important part in the production." Give the letters with the date and time of the first rehearsal to the **older** children only.

The second letter should read: "We are planning a special Christmas program on December ____. The younger children are invited to the rehearsals on _____ in the _____ room of the church." The children with speaking parts will be meeting at an earlier date. The younger children will wait to rehearse until the main characters are ready.

d. It is important to tell the waiting children that they will be needed on a later date so they will anticipate being included. Both letters should encourage parents to attend rehearsals and help out. You will be grateful for the extra hands. If the very young ones, who do not have speaking parts, are included too soon in rehearsals, they become bored and disruptive. Invite them only to the dress rehearsal.

e. Write a child's name on each letter so that if he/she is not in Sunday school that day, the letters can be mailed to the children's homes.

f. Place a notice in the church bulletin on the Sunday after the letters are sent out, to announce the Christmas program with the date and time. Don't forget the church newsletter.

g. It is my feeling that *every* child should be encouraged to be a part of all Sunday school activities. They can be used as angels and shepherds or lambs (with little ears). Often a toddler will steal the show when he comes out in his angel costume with a tinsel halo hanging over one ear, or a mischievous child turns into a serious shepherd just by tagging along after the bigger children. A child may act up at rehearsal, but on the day of the performance, with their parents and friends watching, he usually comes through in an amazing way.

h. Sometimes older boys do not want to be a part of a program. Offer them the opportunity to help with lighting, sets, or props. They can then be involved on their own terms and the program becomes truly a children's production. Junior high children can be used as ushers on the night of the program.

i. Those who attend the first rehearsal are the ones most interested and should receive the better parts (unless the child made an effort to inform the director that he/she cannot attend the first rehearsal but really wants to participate). Be flexible. Drama experience or talent is not necessary; parents will love whatever their child does. Actors do not have to look the part. If the child feels strongly about being involved, the director will have all his/her cooperation. He/she will surprise the director by the special meaning given to the part.

j. After every rehearsal a letter should go home with the children. This letter always states the date and time of the program, plus rehearsal dates and times. The dates for the **dress rehearsal** should appear in bold print so that parents will remember. As time goes on, the letters need to include more information regarding costumes, sets, and what is needed from the parents in the way of props, costumes, or whatever else may be needed. Mention the Christmas party and ask the parents to bring goodies to share. Point out that they may bring family and friends to the production.

k. **Important:** Be sure to give the director's phone number or email address to the parents and request that they contact the director if their child will not be able to participate.

l. Be sure to keep updates and reminders in the Sunday church bulletin and the church newsletter.

5. **Doing The Job**
   a. **The director is in charge.** Be gracious and considerate but do not hesitate to let everyone know what they should be doing. *Without strong leadership nothing gets done.*
   b. Assign a leader to each group of children according to their parts at the first rehearsal. Each group will consist of children who will be performing in the general area where their action takes place (such as shepherds in the field, angels in heaven, the manger scene). The leader assists the children with their parts and is responsible for bringing them in at the right time throughout the rehearsals and presentation of the play.
   c. Each group leader is assigned seating at the back of the room. They will sit with their children at every rehearsal and during the play. Familiarity brings security to nervous actors.
   d. Bring the children together following rehearsal. Encourage them and point out all the good things you see happening. Discuss problems and answer questions about dates, costumes, props, and anything else. If they request it, they may take their scripts home to memorize; otherwise, collect them. Remind them of the next rehearsal date and time and distribute their letters as they leave.
   e. If possible, hold a short meeting of all of the leaders following each rehearsal. Discuss their ideas and suggestions, and anything needing attention. Thank them for their help and remind them that they are needed at *all* rehearsals. Let them know how important they are and remind them that if they need to be away they should see that someone takes their place.
   f. **Costumes, props, and sets:** Do not attempt to do this alone. Parents or someone from the women's or men's groups at the church, friends, or the custodian can be used. Assign adults to work on costumes (old ones can be refurbished, new ones need to be made). Assign one adult and two or more helpers for props or sets that need to be constructed or repaired. The more people become involved, the more interest and excitement is generated.
   g. **Dress rehearsal:** Assign older children to be big brothers or sisters to very young children when they are on stage so they can keep watch over them. This makes it unnecessary for adults to be running into the middle of the production to round up a stray child.
   h. **Announce at the dress rehearsal** that all the children and leaders are to arrive, with costumes in hand, an hour before the program and to meet in the _____ room.
   i. **Do not worry** when rehearsals become chaotic ... they usually are. Join in the fun and laugh, then bring them together again by using all of the leaders and helpers.

6. **The Printed Program**
   a. Prepare a program that includes the title of the program, the name of the pastor, the name of the church, the church's address and phone number, plus the date and time of the program. The inside of the program should include: the title of the program, scripture used, author, director, children's names and roles, a listing of the musicians, production crew, and all of the leaders with a thank you to all who helped.
   b. On the back of the program be sure to invite everyone to the Christmas party in the _____ room. If a home is used for the party, be sure to list both names of the hosts plus a complete address and directions to their home. Do not put anything in the program about bringing goodies. This information is best given in the letters that are sent home and the bulletin announcements prior to the program. Guests often feel awkward about coming if they think they should be bringing something.
   c. Choose carols to sing, and use first verses only.
   d. **Keep the program simple:** There will be babies and other children attending and the place will be alive with activity and excitement.

7. **Presentation**
   a. If carols are to be sung, arrange for a song leader and an accompanist. Is there a young person who plays an instrument? Ask him/her in plenty of time and let him/her select the music he/she wishes to play.
   b. Have Christmas carols playing softly as people enter.
   c. Ask your junior high youth to be ushers and use two at each door to pass out programs. Have an adult handy to be helpful to them and to guide them as is necessary.
   d. In a separate room, before the program, gather the children who have parts around the director. Take care that there are no distractions (such as toys) within their reach. The children should read through the whole play until the director is satisfied.
   e. Leaders will costume little ones as they arrive and then have them join the older children in the circle. Leaders sit with the youngest around the outside of the circle so that they may help keep better control. If a child becomes disruptive, it often helps calm him if an adult touches him lightly on the head or shoulder. Helpers may need to temporarily remove an overexcited child.
   f. It is important to make sure that *every* child goes to the bathroom before entering the area where the program will be put on. Nothing is more embarrassing to everyone than to have to remove a squirming, uncomfortable child.
   g. Each group lines up with their leader. After straightening costumes, combing hair, wiping dirty faces, and being certain the children have gone to the bathroom, the leader then walks them quietly into the sanctuary. This is the peak excitement time. The director should reassure them that they will be great.
   h. Each leader will walk his/her group into the room to sit in their assigned place until time to go on.
   i. The director should plan to sit in the front row — or on the floor where the children can see him/her. A soft blanket or cushion could be placed on the floor so that the director may be comfortable and remain clean. Helpers should sit at each end of the front row with a script to be ready to prompt.
   j. The director will take a bow with the children at the end of the program, so he/she should dress appropriately.
   k. Do not hesitate to remove a child that is acting out.
   l. Speak to each child and all of the parents following the program, and say something nice about the performances.
   m. Attend the Christmas party.

8. **Follow Up**
   a. Everyone will enjoy everything that happens no matter who forgot their lines or made a wrong entrance; children are beautiful. When the children go on stage that magical night, dressed in their costumes, with music, spotlights, and their parents, relatives, and friends out front, they will do their best. The director will feel the pride of every child and parent. It will be a good experience, I promise.
   b. Write a thank-you note to each leader the next week. The director will probably be asked to do this again next year and it is good to have the cooperation of all.
   c. The director should give himself/herself a pat on the back for a job well done!
   d. Please, write to me and tell me all about the program. Doris Wells Miller, 3775 Modoc Road #292, Santa Barbara, California 93105.

Step-By-Step Worksheet

Check off each item as it is completed

1. **Program**
   a. Choose a program in September
   b. Clear dates with the church calendar
   c. Consider ages of the children

2. **Selection**
   a. Prepare the material and scripts
   b. Enlist support

3. **Planning**
   a. Music
   b. Musicians
   c. Assistants
   d. Rehearsals
   e. Party
   f. Recording production

4. **Rehearsals**
   a. Request permission
   b. Read through script
   c. Prepare two letters
   d. Include waiting children
   e. Add names to letters
   f. Place bulletin notice
   g. Use every child
   h. Involve reluctant children
   i. First rehearsal and assignments
   j. Letters after every rehearsal
   k. Give your contact information
   l. Updates and reminders in bulletin and newsletter

5. **Doing The Job**
   a. Be in charge
   b. Assign leaders
   c. Assign seating
   d. Gather children at end of each rehearsal and praise their efforts and answer questions
   e. Leader meeting

   f. Assign helpers to costumes, props, and settings
   g. Dress rehearsal: assign big brothers and sisters
   h. Children arrive before program
   i. Discuss handling chaos

6. **The Printed Program**
   a. Prepare the program
   b. Invite all to the party
   c. Choose carols
   d. Keep it simple

7. **Presentation**
   a. Arrange for accompanist
   b. Music plays as people gather
   c. Ushers at each entrance
   d. Gather children to read parts
   e. Leaders costume little ones, check faces, hair, and everything else
   f. Bathroom time for each child
   g. Groups line up with their leader
   h. Children go to assigned areas
   i. Director sits in front row
   j. Be prepared to take a bow
   k. Remove an unruly child
   l. Speak to each child after the program
   m. Go to the party

8. **Follow Up**
   a. Feel the pride of the children and their parents
   b. Write a thank-you note to all of the helpers
   c. Pat yourself on the back
   d. Write to the author

Synopsis And Stage Directions
For Each Play

Angels We Have Heard

Angels, in costume, gather on the highest part of the stage. Across the front, where the angels stand, are clouds made from cotton pasted on cardboard or painted on blue paper. The area on the lower area, probably your floor, will be earth where several vignettes take place. Following each vignette, the angels discuss what they see and express how they feel about it.

The Play:

The Heavenly Hosts are preparing for the birth of the Son of God. Come with us as we watch Gabriel, the Archangel, deliver God's message to Zechariah, a righteous priest. Gabriel tells Zechariah that even in his old age he will have a son, and he is to name him John. Then behold, Mary, a young girl, is told that she will bear the Son of God.

God sends Gabriel to bring comfort and understanding to Joseph as he struggles with the laws of the Israelites and his love for Mary. Certainly we can share the Angel's happiness as they tell of the Savior's birth and sing the Gloria refrain to the Shepherds out in the fields. We will rejoice with the Angels as we see the coming of Jesus, the Son of God.

Even The Least Among You

The stage is set in three sections. On stage left is a stable with a manger. Center stage serves as the center of town with a well. On the right is the gate to the town of Bethlehem. A podium is on the far side where stands Mary, a reader, a narrator, and an angel who will all take their turns sharing the microphone.

The Play:

A young couple makes the long journey to Bethlehem in response to Caesar's decree that all must return to the city of their ancestors in order to be counted for the census so they can be taxed. Mary, with child, and Joseph, her betrothed, look for a warm bed, but, there was none to be found. The town was full and overflowing with travelers. Finally, giving up hope of finding a room, they were on their way out of town when they met a young man, Matthias, a cripple begging at the city gate, an outcast. Perhaps, because he had known hardship, he was able to see their need and offers the only thing he has, his bed in the stable. Seeing that the time has come for Mary to have her baby, Matthias goes for help. Thinking only of the need of this young couple, he forgets his own affliction and experiences a special healing as he drops his crutch and runs for help.

The Christmas Hedgehog

This is a play within a play. Although it is about real people, the Smith family, used with their permission, the events are *not* true. It takes place late in November, as the Sunday school is preparing for their annual Christmas play. The story is told by an older person, Julie Smith, who is sharing her memories of a Christmas that had a very special meaning to her. **Note:** even the grownups in the Smith family are played by the children.

The Play:

David, Julie's brother, and Jimmy are best friends. Jimmy is experiencing some problems dealing with the attention his new baby sister is getting. Jimmy feels that no one cares about him so he has been giving everyone a hard time, including his best friend, David.

A rehearsal for the Animals' Christmas pageant has just been held and the participants in the play are preparing to leave. Jimmy has again been rebuffed by his mother as everyone makes over his baby sister. He goes back into the church to release his anger and do whatever mischief he can find. Through his friend David's "little talk with Jesus," Jimmy finds understanding and unconditional love and learns that Jesus loves him, too. Forgiveness is given and they go off, arm in arm, to play.

The Magi

The three Wise Men are astronomers. The apprentice is studiously working with his primitive sextant. When the apprentice discovers the new star, a dream and ancient records reveal that it signals the birth of a "Ruler of the Universe." They set off on their journey to find this new king, carrying three valuable gifts. On reaching Jerusalem, they meet a treacherous Herod who tries to trick them. Finding the Christ Child, they return to the East by way of a different route.

The Play:

Caspar, a young apprentice, is measuring the heavens when he sees a new star. His father, Melchior, his instructor, thinks he has made an error. Balthasar has a dream that tells of the birth of a "King of kings." They begin their journey to pay him homage and carry gifts befitting a great king.

When they arrive in Jerusalem, Herod tells them to go to Bethlehem then orders them to return to Jerusalem and tell him where this new king is located. On entering Bethlehem, they find Joseph and Mary and the young child. After presenting their gifts to the child, they are warned in a dream to leave by another route. Herod is very angry when he finds he has been deceived. When the Magi leave, they warn Joseph that he would be wise to leave, too.

Who Is Your King?

Emperor Augustus sits upon his throne. A guard is standing at the Emperor's left and an Advisor on his right. The scepter in his hand is so tall that it stands on the floor.

The Play:

Over 2,000 years ago, Emperor Augustus, ruler of the Roman Empire, decreed that everyone must go to the place of the birth of their ancestor in order to be registered to pay their taxes. Joseph and Mary went to Bethlehem as they were descendants of King David. Upon arrival in Bethlehem, Mary gave birth to God's Son, Jesus. After the birth of the Christ Child there appeared a great star, which foretold the birth of a King. This star was sighted in the East by Wise Men and they recognized the star as a sign of the birth of a King of kings. They immediately made plans to travel to the West to find this King and pay homage and bring him gifts.

When Herod heard their story he was furious with the thought that another King might take his place. He inquired of the scribes and teachers of the law to seek out where this child was to be born. Upon finding out that it was in Bethlehem, Herod told the Wise Men where to find this newborn King and then began to lay plans to destroy him. An angel speaks to the Wise Men in a dream and they leave town by another route.

Where Is Your Lamb?

This play is written for a slightly older group — probably grades 4 through 8. A storyteller and cantor retell the events leading up to the birth of Jesus. The story centers on a shepherd and his family and their trust in God.

The Play:

It has been cold and raining, but the shepherds must take their sheep into the hillsides. It illustrates the dangers a shepherd faces as he leads his sheep. They encounter Joseph and Mary as Joseph finds one of their lost lambs and returns it.

Joseph and Mary go into Bethlehem where the Christ Child is born in a stable. Angels appear to the shepherds and tell of the birth. When he reenters Bethlehem, the shepherd meets his wife, who then joins them in the excitement of seeing the newborn King that the angels told them about. She excitedly runs to tell others in the town.

Angels We Have Heard

And suddenly there was with the angel a multitude of the heavenly host praising God and saying,
"Glory to God in the highest heaven, and on earth peace among those whom he favors!"

— Luke 2:13-14

Characters

Narrator	Angel Seven
Angel One	Mary
Angel Two	Elizabeth (nonspeaking)
Angel Three (Choir Director)	Joseph (nonspeaking)
Angel Six	Shephered One
Angel Four	Shepherd Two
Gabriel	Shepherd Three
Angel Five	Shepherd Four
Zechariah	

(The stage could be fronted with fluffy clouds signifying the Angels moving about heaven. All the Angels are in the Heavenly Choir. Angel Three directs the Angel Choir. They are tuning up their voices, but they don't sound very good. One Angel is strumming a harp. You may use an autoharp or a pretend harp. Mary also needs a doll to portray the baby Jesus and a manger. An altar should be set up to one side.)

Narrator: The Heavenly Hosts are preparing for the birth of the Son of God. Let us experience together their reaction as we share in the joy of this exciting event as God touched man. Come with us as we watch Gabriel, the Archangel, deliver God's message to Zechariah, a righteous priest. He tells Zechariah that even in his old age he will have a son, and he is to name him John. Then behold, as we watch, Mary, a young girl, as she is told that she will bear the Son of God.

God sends Gabriel to bring comfort and understanding to Joseph as he struggles with the laws of the Israelites and his love for Mary. Certainly we can share the Angel's happiness as they tell of the Savior's birth and sing the Gloria refrain to the Shepherds out in the fields. We will rejoice with the Angels as we share in the coming of Jesus, the Son of God.

Angel One: What's going on here?

Angel Two: The Most High just gave us a new song to learn.

(Heavenly Choir sings slowly and not very well, "Gloria," from "Angels We Have Heard On High.")

Angel One: *(walks away from singing Angels with hands still over her ears)* You sound worse than the harpist. *(makes a face)*

Angel Three: The Most High asked us to sing a new song; we are just trying to learn it.

17

Angel One: *(facing audience, hands over ears ... looking desperate)* Is there no place in heaven where I can find some peace and quiet?

(Angels look around as if they hear something, stop practicing and go to edge of heaven where they look down on earth and listen. They look sad.)

Angel Three: *(looking out over earth — the audience)* Listen! Hear how God's people cry out day and night.

Angel Six: It is so sad.

Angel Four: Humans are so cruel to one another.

Angel Six: *(wipes a tear from eye)* It just makes me want to cry.

Angel One: *(crosses arms over chest and pouts)* I guess it *is* better to be in heaven ... even if it is noisy.

(Gabriel enters from stage left. He walks to edge of heaven and looks down on earth and shakes head sadly. Then he turns and speaks to Angels.)

Gabriel: The Most High is sending me down to earth.

Angel Five: What are you going to do, Gabriel?

Gabriel: I am going to deliver a very important message to that old man burning incense at the altar.

(Lights dim. Spot goes to an old man [Zechariah] walking slowly toward an altar.)

Angel Three: Oh, yes, that's Zechariah, he and his wife, Elizabeth, are good people; they have always tried to do what is right.

Angel Five: You are right ... they have always obeyed God's commands.

(Gabriel steps down from heaven and goes over to Zechariah's side. Zechariah, who is lighting incense looks up and sees the Angel. Zechariah steps back, mouth and eyes wide open in surprise and fear.)

Gabriel: Don't be afraid, Zechariah.

Zechariah: Who ... who are you? What are you doing in the holy of holies?

Gabriel: God has heard your prayers, Zechariah. Your wife, Elizabeth, will become pregnant and she will bear a son. You are to name him John.

Zechariah: We? We are to have a child?

Gabriel: And from his birth he will be filled with the Holy Spirit.

Zechariah: A baby? *(pause)* A son?

Gabriel: He will go ahead of the Lord, like the prophet Elijah. He will turn your people back to the way of righteousness.

Zechariah: *(unbelieving)* How ... how can this be?

Gabriel: He will get the Lord's people ready for him.

Zechariah: But, I am an old man. And, my wife is old, too.

Gabriel: I am Gabriel; I stand in the presence of God who sent me.

Zechariah: It cannot be.

Gabriel: You have not believed me, so, you will not be able to speak until the day my promise comes true. *(turns and walks back to heaven leaving a very stunned Zechariah)*

(Back in heaven, the Angels greet Gabriel.)

Angel One: Why, Gabriel? Why wouldn't Zechariah believe you?

Angel Two: Doesn't he know that God is always true?

(Gabriel walks to edge of heaven and looks down at Zechariah trying to talk to the audience by moving his hands and arms about.)

Angel Three: Look at Zechariah. He has to make signs with his hands.

Angel Four: They make it so hard on themselves when they don't believe God.

Angel Five: Poor fellow, no one understands what has happened.

(Spotlight on Zechariah as he walks slowly down the aisle. Angels go back to practicing their song. They are beginning to sound a little better. Lights go down and then up to denote time.)

Narrator: When his period of service in the temple was over, a silent Zechariah went home. Sometime later, his wife, Elizabeth, became pregnant. In the sixth month of Elizabeth's pregnancy, God sent the Angel Gabriel to Nazareth, a town in Galilee. He had a message for a girl promised in marriage to a man named Joseph.

(Gabriel walks to the edge of heaven and starts to go down to earth.)

Angel Six: Gabriel, come over and hear us sing our new song.

Angel Seven: Yes, Gabriel, we have the new song all ready.

Gabriel: Not now my friends, I have to deliver another message.

(Angels watch as Gabriel goes to earth and walks over to a young girl sleeping on a mat.)

Instrumental   "Lo, How A Rose E're Blooming"

Gabriel: *(to Mary)* Peace be with you!

Mary: *(startled ... sits up wide-eyed ... frightened)* Who ... who are you?

Gabriel: Don't be afraid, Mary. God has been gracious to you.

Mary: Are you an Angel?

Gabriel: I have a message for you from the Most High God. You will give birth to a son, and you will name him Jesus.

Mary: *(in wonderment)* But, but how can this be?

Gabriel: God's power will rest on you; the Holy Child shall be called the Son of God.

Mary: *(obediently ... softly)* I am the Lord's servant.

(Angel leaves. Mary pulls blanket up and looks thoughtful, but bewildered.)

Instrumental or Solo   "Lo, How A Rose E're Blooming"

(Lights dim, then go up; denoting time.)

Narrator: Soon afterward, Mary prepared herself and hurried off to the hill country, to a town in Judea to the home of Zechariah and Elizabeth.

(Angels gather around the edge of heaven and look down on earth.)

Angel Three: Look, there goes Mary to visit her cousin, Elizabeth.

Angel Two: Elizabeth can use her help, she is old, and it is hard for her now that she is carrying the baby.

(Mary greets Elizabeth and they embrace.)

Angel Four: Oh, look how happy they are to see one another!

Angel Five: Even the baby jumped for joy....

(Angels clap hands and jump for joy, too.)

Angel Six: *(wipes tear from eye)* It makes me want to cry.

(Lights go down and up to denote time.)

Narrator: The time came for Elizabeth to have her baby and she bore a son. Zechariah was again able to speak and praised God as he named his new son John. He is known to us as "John the Baptist" who announced the coming of our Lord Jesus. Mary then returned home.

Angel Five: *(looking over side of heaven)* Uh-oh.

(The other Angels come over to look.)

Angel Three: What is happening?

Angel Five: Mary is returning home from her visit with Elizabeth.

Angel Four: There's Joseph. He sees her. Uh-oh.

Angel Six: He doesn't look too happy.

Angel One: What will he do?

Angel Two: The Israelites have very strict laws. He could have Mary stoned.

Angel One: *(frightened)* Oh, no ... no.

(When Joseph sees Mary, he turns his back on her and stalks off angrily, and Mary turns and leaves crying. Gabriel goes to the side of heaven to watch, then goes to the back of the stage. Angels continue to watch, looking fearful and worried. Soon Gabriel returns and goes directly to earth. There he sees Joseph sleeping fitfully on a mat.)

Gabriel: *(standing near Joseph's head)* Joseph, descendant of David.

(Joseph remains asleep, with his head turned toward Gabriel and the audience with eyes closed.)

Gabriel: Do not be afraid to take Mary as your wife for she is with child by the Holy Spirit. She will have a son, and you will name him Jesus, and he will save his people from their sins.

(Angel returns to heaven. Joseph smiles in his sleep. Other Angels greet Gabriel with relief. Lights go down and then up to denote time.)

Narrator: Joseph and Mary had gone to Bethlehem as they were required by the Emperor to register themselves for the taxes in the town of their ancestor. When they arrived, the town was so crowded that there was no room for them in the inn, and they had to find shelter in a cave among the animals. In time, it came to pass in the city of David, the town of Bethlehem, the Christ Child was born.

(Mary holds baby, Joseph stands by her side, Angels are excited.)

(Angel Choir sings "Silent Night.")

(Angels Two and Three go to earth to the area of the room where Shepherds are lying down with their sheep.)

Angel Two: Glory be to God!

(Shepherds wake up, look around frightened.)

Angel Three: Don't be afraid.

Shepherd One: Who are you?

Angel Two: We bring good news.

Angel Three: Which will bring great joy to all people.

Shepherd Two: What's going on?

Angel One: This very day, in David's town, your Savior is born.

Shepherd Three: Who? Where?

Angel Three: Christ the Lord, your Messiah.

Shepherd Four: How will we find him?

Angel Two: You will find the baby wrapped in swaddling cloths and lying in a manger.

(The other Angels have quietly surrounded the Shepherds and begin to sing the "Gloria" from "Angels We Have Heard On High" that they have been practicing.)

Shepherd One: Let us go to Bethlehem.

Shepherd Two: And see this thing that has happened.

Shepherd Three: Which the Heavenly Hosts have told us.

(Shepherds walk to front where manger is and bow before Jesus. Angels circle behind the Nativity and sing the "Gloria" refrain.)

The End

Even The Least Among You

And all in the crowd were trying to touch him, for power came out from him and healed all of them.
— Luke 6:19

Characters

Narrator	Matthias
Reader	Philip *(shepherd)*
Angel	Cyrus *(shepherd)*
Mary	Nathaniel *(shepherd)*
Sarah	Anne
Esther	Joseph

Scene One

(The stage is set in three sections. On the left front is a stable with a manger. Center stage serves as the center of town with a well. On the right is the gate to the town of Bethlehem. A podium is on the side, where Mary, a Reader, a Narrator, and an Angel share the same microphone.)

Narrator: A young couple makes the long journey to Bethlehem in response to Caesar's decree that all must return to the city of their ancestors in order to be counted for the census so they could be taxed. Mary, with child, and Joseph, her betrothed, looked for a warm bed for the night, but, there was none. The town was full and overflowing. Finally, giving up hope of finding a room, they were on their way out of town when they met a young man, Matthias, begging at the city gate crippled, and an outcast. Perhaps because he had known hardship, he was able to see their need and offers the only thing he has, his bed in the stable. Seeing that the time has come for Mary to have her baby, Matthias goes for help. Thinking only of the need of this young couple, he forgets his own affliction and experiences a special healing as he drops his crutch and runs for help. Through the years, he continues to be good friends of this special family and eventually becomes a devoted follower of Jesus.

Reader: In the sixth month the angel Gabriel was sent by God to a town in Galilee called Nazareth, to a virgin engaged to a man whose name was Joseph, of the house of David. The virgin's name was Mary (Luke 1:26-27).

Angel: Greetings, favored one! The Lord is with you.

Reader: But she was much perplexed by his words and pondered what sort of greeting this might be (Luke 1:29).

Angel: Do not be afraid, Mary, for you have found favor with God. And now, you will conceive in your womb and bear a son, and you will name him Jesus. He will be great, and will be called the Son of the Most High, and the Lord God will give to him the throne of his ancestor David. He will reign over the house of Jacob forever, and of his kingdom there will be no end (Luke 1:30-33).

Mary: How can this be, since I am a virgin? (Luke 1:34).

23

Angel: The Holy Spirit will come upon you, and the power of the Most High will overshadow you; therefore the child to be born will be holy; he will be called Son of God (Luke 1:35).

Choir "Come, Thou Long Expected Jesus" (v. 1)

Reader: In those days a decree went out from Emperor Augustus that all the world should be registered for the paying of their taxes. All went to their own towns to be registered. Joseph also went from the town of Nazareth in Galilee to Judea, to the city of David called Bethlehem, because he was descended from the house and family of David (Luke 2:1-4).

Narrator: Bethlehem was a town of shepherds. The ancestral birthplace of David, son of Jesse. A small town, yet destined to be great for it was the birthplace of Jesus, the Son of God. Come, let us once again relive that awesome time. It is dawn and the women of the town begin their day by coming to the well to draw water.

(Esther enters with a jar on her head and goes to the well to draw water. She lowers her jar, on a rope, into the well, then pulls it up and sits to rest on the rim of the well. Sarah enters with a jug from right aisle. At the same time, Matthias, who is sleeping on the straw in the stable [left stage], awakens and struggles to his feet with the help of a crude crutch. He hangs a cup, which is fastened to a thong, around his neck and begins his slow, awkward walk to the well.)

Sarah: Good morning, Esther.

Esther: Oh, good morning, Sarah.

Sarah: There is a chill in the air this morning.

Esther: I do hope it isn't going to rain again; we have had more than enough.

Matthias: *(finally reaching the well)* Good morning. Would one of you please pour some water into my cup?

(Esther and Sarah try to ignore Matthias.)

Matthias: I am very thirsty and have no way to draw the water. Could not one of you share a cup of water with me?

Sarah: *(lets her jug down into the well and then draws it up and pours water into Matthias' cup)* Very well.

Matthias: *(drinks from the cup then starts to make his slow, awkward walk to the city gate at stage right)* Thank you, Sarah.

(Philip and Cyrus enter with botas over their shoulders, going up left aisle toward the well.)

Philip: Good morning, neighbors, may we draw some water to fill our botas?

Cyrus: We are on our way to the fields to the north to watch the flocks.

Sarah: Yes, you may. Here, use my jug.

(The men let the jug into the water and begin to fill their botas.)

Nathaniel: *(enters with bota from center aisle)* Greetings, friends, are you ready to leave for the fields?

Cyrus: Just as soon as we fill our botas. There is enough water in this jar to fill yours, too.

(They fill their botas and hang them across their shoulders.)

Philip: So long, my friends.

Cyrus: I for one am glad we are going to the fields, this town is too crowded for me.

Nathaniel: We have allowed a family to stay in our upper room; there was no room in the inn.

Philip: We would have rented our room, too, except with all our children we just did not have any extra space. We certainly could have used the money to pay the taxes.

Anne: *(enters from left aisle)* Good morning. It looks as if the weather is clearing and the sun will shine today.

Cyrus: It is a good thing. We are heading north into the hills to look after the sheep.

Philip: The nights will be cold, but it is worse when it rains.

Nathaniel: We must be going, or we will never reach the field before dark.

(Cyrus, Philip, and Nathaniel gather their gear and start for the city gate.)

Choir   "As Joseph Was A'walking"

(Matthias has reached the gate and sits against the wall in his accustomed place. He holds out his cup to ask for alms. A young couple enter by walking slowly up the right aisle. They pass Matthias as they enter.)

Matthias: Alms ... alms for the poor. Have mercy on a poor cripple.

Joseph: *(reaching into his pack, he takes a coin out and places it in the cup)* Good morning, young man. God's blessing on you this day.

Matthias: Good morning to you. Thank you and God's blessing on you, too.

(Joseph and Mary head toward the well where Esther, Sarah, and Anne are chatting. Cyrus, Philip, and Nathaniel are on their way out of the city and pass by the young couple.)

Nathaniel: *(shakes head sadly then speaks to his friends)* Another family is arriving.

Cyrus: We can't get out of this town fast enough to suit me.

Joseph: Kind sirs, could you tell us where the inn is located?

Philip: The end of town, but, it will do you no good. It has been full for a week.

(Cyrus, Philip, and Nathaniel move out the city gate where they ignore Matthias' request for alms. Joseph and Mary reach the well and they pause to draw water.)

Joseph: Good morning, ladies. May we draw water from the well to fill our bota?

Esther: *(moves aside)* If you must.

Mary: We thank you kindly.

Anne: I suppose you are here to register for the taxes.

Joseph: Yes, both Mary and I are from the family of David. As you can see it was a bad time for us to make this trip. Mary is with child and the trip has been hard on her.

Anne: You do look tired, my child. This is certainly not a good time for you to travel, here, sit on the side of the well and rest.

Mary: *(sits on the rim of the well as Joseph takes a bota from his shoulder, Anne puts a small jug into the well and brings it up to fill their bota)* Thank you for your kindness.

Joseph: The shepherds say that the inn is full. Do you know where we might stay tonight?

Esther: There is no room in town. We have a family staying with us as do many of the people in town. You may as well turn around and stay somewhere outside the gate.

Mary: I do not think I will be able to do that as I feel that the child is due any time.

Anne: You poor dear. If I knew of any place I would tell you, but every room is full.

Joseph: We shall still have to try. Come, Mary, let us go to the inn and see if anyone has left.

(Joseph and Mary begin their weary way down the center aisle.)

Esther: Curse Caesar, sending all these strangers into our town just so he will get more taxes.

Sarah: Take care how you speak of mighty Caesar. He is dangerous.

Anne: It just isn't fair. Everything was so peaceful until now.

Esther: My family is probably wondering where I am. I had better get home.

Sarah: Yes, my children will be looking for me, too.

Anne: So long, my friends.

(The women head back to their homes the way they entered. When they are gone, Joseph and Mary walk slowly up the center aisle to the well.)

Joseph: Oh, Mary, I am so sorry. You are so tired and we have nowhere to stay, I don't know what to do.

Mary: It is not your fault, my dear Joseph.

(Mary sits on side of well. Joseph offers Mary a drink of water.)

Joseph: Well, it is certain that we cannot stay in town.

(Joseph and Mary wearily adjust their belongings and start for the city gate. Matthias is still at the gate begging for alms.)

Matthias: Good people, you are leaving so soon?

Joseph: There was no room at the inn.

Mary: And the women at the well said that there were no rooms left in town.

Joseph: We did stop at several homes to inquire, but they all turned us away.

Matthias: You must be very tired.

Joseph: Yes, we can go no further.

Matthias: *(thinking to himself)* It is only a stable among the animals, but it is warm and the straw is soft. *(to Joseph)* Dear friends, my bed is poor, but, warm. Would you care to come home with me?

Joseph: Yes, yes. We would be ever so grateful!

Mary: Bless you! You are so kind.

(Matthias, Joseph, and Mary turn toward town again, and they make their slow journey past the well and to the stable where Matthias shows Mary his crude bed. Joseph spreads his cloak on the straw and helps Mary sit down.)

Matthias: I will go find Anne, she is the midwife. I know she will help.

(Matthias begins his awkward way up the center aisle, but, within a few steps, he slowly straightens up and stands a second, then drops his crutch to the ground. He continues joyously up the center aisle and soon returns bringing Anne with him.)

Scene Two

Choir   "Gentle Mary Laid Her Child" (v. 1)

Reader: While they were there, the time came for her to deliver her child. And she gave birth to her firstborn son and wrapped him in bands of cloth, and laid him in a manger, because there was no place for them in the inn (Luke 2:6-7).

(On far right of the stage the Shepherds are asleep on the ground. Their sheep are scattered among them. You can use toy sheep or cardboard cutouts or dress the youngest children in white caps with long white ears.)

Narrator: There, in the still of the night, Mary brought forth her firstborn child and wrapped him in swaddling clothes. At that time, while the shepherds were keeping watch over their flocks, a wonderful thing happened. The heavenly hosts brought the good news to the humble men in the fields as they tended their sheep. The angels sang, "Gloria, peace on earth to all men of good will." Awakening, the shepherds were frightened but the angels told them not to fear, that their Savior, Christ the Lord, had been born in a stable in the town of Bethlehem. The shepherds immediately arose and returned to the town to find the child spoken of by the angels.

Choir   "Gentle Mary Laid Her Child" (v. 2)

(Carrying their sheep, or guiding the children dressed as sheep, the Shepherds get up and walk through the city gate and stop at the well.)

Philip: Have we been dreaming? Did we actually hear God's angels singing to us?

Cyrus: It happened! I know it did!

Nathaniel: Yes, the angel spoke to us. He said that somewhere in this town the Messiah has been born. We have to find him.

Philip: The angel said a ... a manger?

Cyrus: He is our Lord. Why would God's Son be found in a stable?

Philip: That's it, the stable. That's what the angel said. That is where we will find him.

(The Shepherds excitedly make their way to the stable and look in to see the Holy Family.)

Nathaniel: May we come in?

Cyrus: There he is. The babe is here.

Joseph: Come in, my friends, come in.

Choir   "Good Christian Men Rejoice" (v. 1)

Nathaniel: Angels came to us in the field.

Philip: They told us that the Messiah, the Son of God, was born this night and we would find him lying in a manger, wrapped in swaddling cloths.

Narrator: As the shepherds entered and bowed before the sleeping child, they told of the awesome and wonderful experience they had had in the fields. They told of what the Angel had said about the Christ Child.

Angel: "Do not be afraid; for see — I am bringing you good news of great joy for all the people: to you is born this day in the city of David a Savior, who is the Messiah, the Lord. This will be a sign for you; you will find a child wrapped in bands of cloth and lying in a manger." And suddenly there was with the angel a multitude of the heavenly host, praising God and saying, "Glory to God in the highest heaven, and on earth peace among those whom he favors" (Luke 2:10-14).

Narrator: Mary listened quietly and pondered it all in her heart. It was then that Joseph came to fully understand who this child was that was put into his care. Matthias realized then how he had been given a gift from the Son of God, and his life was changed forever. He went on to live the rest of his life as a follower of Jesus.

The End

The Christmas Hedgehog

Characters

Older Julie	Mrs. Wells
Jerry	Mrs. Malby
Elaine	Mary (nonspeaking)
Deena	Joseph (nonspeaking)
Julie	Donkey
Alice	Dog
Baby	Shepherds (two or three, nonspeaking)
David	Sheep (several, nonspeaking)
Jimmy	

Scene One

(Five chairs are placed in the middle front of the stage in the formation of an imaginary car. A manger scene is located at the center back of the stage. A ladder and greenery need to be placed on the far side of the manger scene. Older Julie stands at a lectern with a microphone at far right stage.)

Older Julie: I remember all my Christmases as being happy times. The holidays were filled with friends and family, the Sunday school program, the Christmas tree and presents, and the delicious food. There have been many Christmases that were special in my life, but, every time I see the manger with the baby Jesus there is one Christmas that stands out in my memory. Tonight, I would like to share it with you. It was a Sunday, just following church. Near Thanksgiving, as I recall.

(Jerry is standing by the car. Elaine has arrived with little Deena and Julie each holding one of her hands.)

Jerry: Where's David? We need to get home right now, the game has already started.

Elaine: I couldn't find him in the classroom.

Jerry: Deena, go find your brother.

(Deena runs back to church, Julie gets into the car. Alice walks up carrying her new baby and greets the family.)

Alice: Hello, Elaine, Jerry. I'm sorry I missed choir last Thursday. Joannie was being very fussy.

Elaine: You were missed. There are so few altos, and we are preparing our Christmas music.

Alice: I'll try to make it next week. By the way, may we borrow your travel crib over the holidays? We are planning a trip to Mother's for Thanksgiving.

Elaine: Why, of course, Alice. Keep it as long as you like; we aren't using it anymore.

31

Jerry: By the way, we have not seen you and John for a long time. Why don't you plan to have dinner with us this Friday, about 6:30?

Alice: We would enjoy that very much, we'll be there. Thank you.

(Deena runs up with David and his friend, Jimmy — their clothes look torn apart.)

Deena: I found them fighting on the playground again.

Elaine: Oh, David, your new pants are ruined.

David: Jimmy pushed me off the swing.

Jerry: *(impatiently)* Well, get in the car so we can go home.

Alice: *(pulling him toward her)* Oh, Jimmy, why did you do that?

Elaine: It's okay, Alice. I'll get the crib over to you in the morning.

(The familys get into the car: Deena, David, and Julie in the backseat, Jerry is driving and Elaine sits next to him. They wave at people as they leave, and everyone pretends to be traveling. They sway with the curves ... look out the windows, like a car ride.)

David: Will you put a band-aid on my knee, Mommy?

Elaine: Yes, dear, when we get home.

Jerry: Why were you and Jimmy fighting? I thought you were best friends.

Elaine: *(reaches over and taps father on the arm)* Now, Jerry.

David: Daddy, what's a deadhog?

Jerry: A deadhog? I've never heard of a deadhog.

Deena: He means a hedgehog, Daddy.

Jerry: Oh, a hedgehog is a small animal, much like a raccoon. Why do you ask?

David: 'Cause, Mrs. Wells wants me to be a deadhog in the Christmas play.

Jerry: I don't understand. What does a hedgehog have to do with Christmas?

Julie: We're doing "The Animals' Christmas," and everyone in the play is an animal.

Elaine: Oh, and what animal are you, Julie?

Julie: I'm the goat that sits in the doorway and talks to the dog.

Deena: And I'm the cow that gave Mary her bed so that she would be able to get some rest.

David: And Jimmy is the lamb.

Deena: *(sneeringly)* Some lamb.

Elaine: Now, Deena, try to think how Jimmy feels. Everyone makes over his baby sister so much, he must feel bad.

David: *(pouting)* But, he's so mean to me.

(They arrive home. Jerry stops the car. Everyone responds bodily to the auto's stopping by swaying back and then forward.... The family leaves car and goes into house.)

Scene Two

(This scene takes place in the stable. There is a small chair in the stable so the Cow can sit on the chair then later gives it to Mary. The Cow and the Hedgehog snuggle close. The Goat sits next to the Dog in the doorway. If possible, it is nice to have a pretend doorway. It could be painted cardboard.)

Older Julie: *(from podium)* A few weeks later, on a Saturday morning, everyone was at the first dress rehearsal for the Christmas play, "The Animals' Christmas." Everyone was in costume and ...

Mrs. Wells: *(bustling about getting everyone arranged, changes her mind and moves children around, then she stands back to direct the children)* All right, children, let's take it from page two.

Mrs. Malby: The friendly dog bounced out to meet the couple as they came down the path and led them to the stable. The man looked into the mouth of the cave and saw the small, warm room. The cow struggled to her feet and offered the tired woman her bed.

Cow: Moooo. She looks so tired ... she shall have my bed.

Mrs. Malby: The man led Mary to the cow's soft bed, spread a blanket, and gently helped his wife, Mary, onto the soft straw. The little cow sighed as she laid herself awkwardly on the hard ground.

(Cow sighs and sits next to the chair and the Hedgehog.)

Donkey: Thank you for giving my mistress your bed.

Cow: Mooooo, I was glad I was able to.

(Mrs. Wells walks over and moves a child so he can be seen better.)

Mrs. Malby: Once more, the animals settle down with the cow now sleeping on the cold, hard ground and the hedgehog curled up close to keep warm. The frisky goat and the dog, sitting near the mouth of the cave, begin to wonder about the strangeness of the night.

Dog: Rrrrufff, I have never seen the stars so bright.

Goat: Aaaaa, nor I, and I've noticed something else, everything is so still, not a sound. This must be a very special night.

Dog: Look, the lights at the inn are down, but it is still so bright.

Mrs. Wells: *(walks over to hand Mary a doll and on her way back she turns the spotlight toward the stable, then moves a few children and animals around so they can be seen better)* That's better. You may go on now, Mrs. Malby.

Mrs. Malby: No one else knew of what was taking place but those within the humble stable. *(pause)* As Mary held the newborn babe, the cow nudged the donkey.

Cow: My manger would make a soft, warm bed for the little one.

Donkey: You are very kind. I'll let my master know what to do. Master ... master. *(touches Joseph on the arm with his nose)*

(Joseph takes doll from Mary and lays it in the manger.)

Mrs. Malby: As the doves cooed the tiny babe to sleep, the animals crowded close to keep each other warm. The dog and goat continue their watch over the night.

(Mrs. Wells dims lights on inside of cave, then turns spotlight on the doorway.)

Dog: What is that up there? *(points his nose to a star in the distance)*

Goat: Aaaaaa star ... the brightest star I've ever seen....

Choir or instrumental   "Do You See What I See?"

Mrs. Malby: Out in the field where the shepherds were tending their flock there were angels who suddenly appeared and told of the great event. The shepherds left the fields and started toward Bethlehem.

(Shepherds and Jimmy, the lamb, come down the aisle, this includes all other little children playing lambs.)

Mrs. Malby: The shepherds arrived leading their flock and entered the stable to kneel before the manger. The lamb poked his head into the doorway and looked around.

(Mrs. Wells adjusts the spotlight on the cave where the manger is located.)

Hedgehog: Go away ... it's already too crowded. We don't need any more animals in here.

Lamb: We would like to see the baby. See the blanket my master carries over his shoulder? It is made from my wool. Let me remind him of what he is to do.

Mrs. Malby: The lamb moves to the manger and tugs at the blanket on the shepherd's shoulder to remind him to give it to the baby. The shepherd removes his shawl and hands it to Mary. She gives him a grateful smile and tucks the warm blanket around the infant.

Mrs. Wells: *(directing)* That's all for today, children. Now be sure to be here next Saturday at 4:30 with your costumes on. See you then.

(As the children leave, little Julie takes her costume off and drops it in the aisle as she rushes for the door. Mrs. Wells and Mrs. Malby greet Alice who comes in with the baby. They stand and chat and fuss over Jimmy's baby sister.)

Mrs. Wells: Isn't she the sweetest thing. May I hold her?

Alice: *(hands baby to Mrs. Wells)* Of course.

(Jimmy runs over to his mother and hangs onto her skirt. Alice pats Jimmy on the head, rather impatiently. Alice walks out with Mrs. Malby and Mrs. Wells, who is holding the baby, as they continue to chat. Jimmy stands alone for a moment and then runs back into the church, picks up the doll in the manger, tears the blanket away, and spanks the doll then throws it back into the manger — upside down. He goes to the side of the stage and climbs a ladder leading to greens used as decorations, above the stable, where he proceeds to tear them apart and throw some onto the floor. David walks back into the sanctuary; he does not see Jimmy, but sees the doll upside down. He picks it up and gently rewraps the doll in the blanket. Julie comes in the side door to pick up her costume that she left on the floor. She stops when she sees David and watches quietly from the side aisle, out of his sight but where the audience can see her.)

David: *(sitting down at front of stage, holding and talking to the doll)* Hi, Jesus.

(Music plays softly in the background.)

David: Jesus, Mrs. Malby tells me in Sunday school that you love everyone.

(Jimmy looks down from his hiding place.)

David: Do you love Jimmy?

(Jimmy shakes his head no.)

David: He has been bad to me, lately. He hits me all the time and calls me names.

Jimmy: *(puts hand over his mouth)* Oh!

David: He has not been very nice to me, but, I still love him ... he's my best friend.

Jimmy: *(tentatively)* Hi, David.

David: *(looks around)* Where are you?

Jimmy: Here I am, up here.

(Jimmy climbs down and sits next to David.)

Jimmy: I'm sorry, I've been so mean, will you be my friend again?

David: *(puts arm around Jimmy)* Of course, Jimmy, come home with me and I'll show you my new airplane.

Jimmy: Okay.

(The boys walk out together, arms around each other.)

Older Julie: I understood right then. It is people loving people that makes the difference. It is Jesus working through our love that causes people to change.

The End

The Magi

Where is the child who has been born king of the Jews? For we observed his star at its rising, and have come to pay him homage.

— Matthew 2:2

Characters

Reader   Baby

Narrator   Herod

Caspar   Darian

Melchior   Chief Priest

Balthasar   Toddler

Mary   Angel

Joseph

Scene One

(A young man sits on a stool in the center of the stage. He has before him a crude measuring instrument that looks like a sextant with a long string attached. In his hand is a tablet on which he writes. Off to the right is a curtain from which Melchior and Balthasar appear. An elevated area is located at far stage left with a small spotlight for the dream sequence.)

Instrumental Music   "Brightest And Best"

Reader: In the East, a young apprentice astronomer discovers the "Star of Bethlehem." When the Wise Men reasoned out that this star was announcing the birth of a "Ruler of the Universe," they set out with their gifts to visit this king, and pay him homage. When they arrive in Jerusalem and inquire of Herod regarding this new king, they receive a rather strange reception. When they find that this king was to have been born in Bethlehem, they set out to find him. Since the Wise Men from the East have been traveling for a long time since first sighting the star, they find a young child, Jesus, living with his family in Joseph's carpenter shop.

Upon discovering the whereabouts of Jesus, they present their gifts to him. The Wise Men, warned in a dream that Herod intends to destroy the child, leave immediately by another route and warn Joseph to do the same.

Narrator: Somewhere in the East, a young apprentice diligently plots the heavens.

(Caspar sits on a stool using an instrument and marks on a chart. He is very intent on his activity. Melchior comes from behind a curtain.)

Melchior: *(kindly)* Now, son, have you worked out your chart yet? *(studies chart, then frowns)* I cannot understand how a young man as intelligent as you, could be so careless. Why can't you plot the distance between two stars? How could you come up with a star in between? It's unthinkable!

Caspar: But, Father, I have plotted the distances three times, and always, it is the same. I don't know what I am doing wrong!

Melchior: *(looking at chart and shaking his head)* This is all wrong. I don't understand. Your figures are correct between Saturn and Jupiter, but just why did you put this star in between?

Caspar: Because that is what I see. Here, Father, look for yourself.

(Melchior reluctantly steps over to the sextant and repeats the measurements.)

Balthasar: *(comes into room and bows lightly to Melchior)* Good morning, master. Caspar, let me tell you about the dream I had last night. It was so real ... as if the Almighty were speaking to me.

Caspar: A dream, Balthasar? What was it about?

Melchior: *(looking through sextant)* Mumble, mumble, mumble ...

Balthasar: There was a beautiful woman and she was very young. She was holding a baby. A man stood beside her with his arms about her shoulders. They were dressed — dressed as ordinary Judeans, but, there was a special glow about them. There were angels singing all around them and a great, bright star above them.

Instrumental or Choir   "Brightest And Best" (v. 1)

Caspar: A baby?

Melchior: A star?

Balthasar: And angels were singing.

Caspar: What could it mean?

Melchior: *(moving away from sextant and looking serious)* A star? A baby? This is a great mystery. *(shakes his head)* Son, you were right. There is a new star in the heavens ... very large and bright. One I have never seen before.

Balthasar: Could the new star be the one in my dream?

Melchior: I shall go into the room of wisdom and see what the ancients have said. Now, Caspar, Balthasar, chart where that star is in relation to the earth. *(strides from the room)*

Balthasar: Caspar, write down these figures as I chart the heavens.

(They busily plot and figure. Looking through the sextant, they both try to be in the same place at the same time. Caspar pops up under Balthasar and gets tangled in the string.)

Melchior: *(returns with scroll from the back room)* I have found it! There is an old and established belief, that it is fated, a man from Judea will rule the world. "You will rule over many nations, but they will not rule over you" (Deuteronomy 15:6b).

Caspar: Ruler of the whole world? Could this be the meaning of my dream?

Balthasar: Certainly, now it makes sense.

Melchior: *(with authority)* We must go to see this king and pay him homage. We shall begin preparations for the trip. Balthasar, have you learned where we should look?

Balthasar: It is in the west, in the land of Judah.

Caspar: Can I go, Father? I found the new star ... oh, Father, I want to go ... I *have* to go with you.

Melchior: It is a long and dangerous journey, my son, but, very well, get your things together. *(turning to Balthasar)* Now Balthasar, prepare provisions and notify the king's guards to establish a caravan. I shall go to the treasury house and select gifts suitable for a king.

(All go in different directions. Caspar returns with a bag and puts on his cape. The others return dressed in their kingly robes, each carrying a traveling bag. They leave, going down the center aisle. Melchior leads, Balthasar next, and finally Caspar properly walking behind the others.)

Scene Two

(Spotlight on a manger scene at left stage area.)

Instrumental   "We Three Kings" (v. 1)

(A chair is placed on center stage [the fanciest one you can find] and Herod takes his place on his throne. Magi walk slowly up aisle with Caspar walking eagerly in front. They pause midway down the aisle.)

Melchior: *(pointing to where King Herod is seated on a throne)* It is only proper that we first seek out the ruler of the Judeans.

Caspar: Father, the star is not over Jerusalem; it is to the south.

Balthasar: Melchior, the chart clearly shows ...

Melchior: It is customary to consult with the present ruler before entering his country. We shall go to Jerusalem.

(They approach the throne of Herod. His advisor stands beside him. Herod stomps his scepter on the floor and whispers to Darian, his advisor.)

Darian: Herod, our esteemed ruler, allows you to approach the throne.

Herod: *(threateningly)* Who are you? Where do you come from? What do you want?

Melchior: *(bowing before Herod)* Herod, O wise and great ruler of Judea. We come in peace. Our names are Melchior, Balthasar, and Caspar. We are from the tribe of Mede of the Empire of Persia.

Balthasar: We have seen a new star. A beautiful, brilliant, and exciting star. And we have had a vision of a newborn king who will rule the whole world.

Caspar: And we have come to worship him and pay homage.

Melchior: Could you tell us where this new king could be?

Herod: *(angrily, to Darian, his advisor)* A new king? In Judea? Why have I not heard of this before?

(Darian looks surprised and frightened, then shrugs his shoulders.)

Herod: Darien. You are my chief advisor. Why have you not told me?

Darian: Herod, O great, wise ruler. Let us consult with the Chief Priest and see what he has to say.

Herod: So be it.

(Darian leaves and returns with the Chief Priest.)

Chief Priest: *(bows low)* O Herod, great ruler, you have sent for me?

Herod: *(angrily)* What is this I hear about a new king being born in Judea?

Chief Priest: O, great one. The scriptures say *(unrolls scroll)*, "And you, Bethlehem, in the land of Judah, are by no means least among the rulers of Judah; for from you will come a ruler who is to shepherd my people Israel" (Matthew 2:6).

Herod: *(pointing to Melchior)* You. Yes, you're the one. Come up here.

Melchior: Yes? O great ruler.

Herod: *(cunningly)* And, just when did this star first appear?

Melchior: We began our trip as soon as we could get a caravan together after my son, Caspar, discovered the new star. We have been traveling for several months.

Herod: *(smiling craftily and rubbing hands together)* Bethlehem is spoken of as the birthplace of a ruler. Go and make a careful search for the child. And, if ... when, you find him, return and tell me all about it so that *(smiling with an evil look)* ... so that I too may go and worship him. Heh heh.

(Magi leave, going down right aisle with Melchior leading. The lights dim.)

Scene Three
(Herod's throne is replaced by a table at which Joseph is hammering on a piece of wood.)

Instrumental   "We Three Kings" (v. 2)

(Magi march back up the left aisle — Caspar eagerly leading the group. They meet Joseph working at a carpenter's table.)

Caspar: Good morning, sir.

Joseph: Greetings strangers. Have you just arrived in town?

Balthasar: We have come a long way and are very tired. Do you know of an inn close by?

Joseph: The inn is at the other end of town, but we would consider it an honor if you would stay in our humble home while you are in Bethlehem.

Caspar: Yes, Father. Could we? Could we?

Melchior: Thank you for your generous offer. We will be pleased to do that.

(Joseph leads the way as Caspar and the others enter the house.)

Joseph: Mary, we have guests. Prepare one of your fine meals and prepare the spare room.

Mary: *(to Caspar who enters first)* Greetings, young man. You are a stranger in Bethlehem. What is your name?

Caspar: Good morning, ma'am. My name is Caspar.

Melchior: *(striding up to the door and bowing lightly)* Greetings. I am Melchior, master of the study of the universe. And this is my assistant, Balthasar, and my son and apprentice, Caspar. We are from the tribe of Mede, from Persia.

(The men make themselves comfortable around the table. Caspar and the toddler [about a year and a half old], sit on the floor where they play quietly. Mary brings out the meal.)

Joseph: Have you been traveling very long?

Balthasar: We began our journey several months ago.

Melchior: We made this trip to find a very special child that is destined to rule the universe.

Balthasar: We saw his star and it led to your village.

Caspar: Do you know of such a child?

Joseph: Mary was visited by God's angel who told her that she would be wonderfully blessed.

Mary: The angel said: "Do not be afraid, Mary, for you have found favor with God. And now, you will conceive in your womb and bear a son, and you will name him Jesus. He will be great, and will be called the Son of the Most High, and the Lord God will give to him the throne of his ancestor David. He will reign over the house of Jacob forever, and of his kingdom there will be no end" (Luke 1:30b-33). The town was crowded so we could not find a room at the inn. The good innkeeper allowed us to stay in his stable behind the inn where Jesus was born.

Joseph: The night that Jesus was born we were visited by Shepherds. They had come from the fields. They told us that Angels had appeared before them and had told them, "Do not be afraid; for see — I am bringing you good news of great joy for all the people: to you is born this day in the city of David a Savior, who is the Messiah, the Lord" (Luke 2:10b-11). And that is how the shepherds found him.

Instrumental *(played softly throughout scene)*   "We Three Kings"

(Magi bow before child.)

Melchior: We are honored to have found him. We have brought gifts we wish to give the king.

(Balthasar goes to side and retrieves his bag and returns to hand out his gifts. He gives one each to Melchior and Caspar and one for himself.)

Melchior: *(lays gift beside child then bows low)* To the ruler of the universe, I bring gold.

Balthasar: *(lays gift beside the child then bows low)* For the light that shines upon the nations ... accept this myrrh as my gift.

Caspar: *(lays gift beside child then bows low)* To the Lord of mercy and grace, I offer frankincense.

Angel: *(from side stage)*   "Come, Thou Long Expected Jesus" by Charles Wesley, 1744
      Come, Thou long expected Jesus,
      Born to set Thy people free;
      From our fears and sins release us;
      Let us find our rest in Thee.
      Israel's strength and consolation,
      Hope of all the earth Thou art;
      Dear Desire of every nation,
      Joy in every longing heart.

(Spotlight goes to an elevated area where Herod is standing, a sword in his hand. Lights go out and then on to symbolize time. Each person enters beginning with Caspar who sits on floor with the child. The others sit at the table, Mary brings breakfast.)

Balthasar: *(seriously)* I had a dream last night. Your ruler, Herod, was very angry. He was shouting and acting like a mad man waving a sword above his head.

Caspar: Oh, how awful ...

Joseph: What could it mean?

Melchior: We have been warned. Herod seeks to destroy the holy child. He fears his throne.

Caspar: Oh no, not Jesus.

Melchior: We shall leave immediately by way of the south. We shall not go near Jerusalem. Herod shall never know.

Balthasar: Caspar, come help me prepare for the journey.

(Mary picks up Jesus. Balthasar and Caspar go out together.)

Melchior: Joseph, you should consider finding a safer place to live.

Joseph: You may be right. We shall prepare to leave immediately.

(All return with bags, say their farewells and leave, going back down left aisle. They get halfway down the aisle when Caspar stops, sets down his bag, turns to look back, and waves at Jesus.)

The End

Who Is Your King?

Characters

Emperor

Guard

Advisor

Narrator

Drummer

Joseph

Mary

Baby

Reader

First Wise Man

Second Wise Man

Third Wise Man

Herod

Ahaz

Priest One

Priest Two

Teacher One

Teacher Two

Teacher Three

Angel One

Angel Two

Scene One

(Emperor Augustus sits upon his throne on stage right. A bright, gold-colored cloth could be placed over a chair to make it look like a throne. A Guard is standing at the Emperor's left and an Advisor on his right. The scepter in his hand is so tall that it stands upon the floor.)

Narrator: Over 2,000 years ago, Emperor Augustus, ruler of the Roman Empire, decreed that every man must go to the place of the birth of their ancestor in order to be registered for the paying of their taxes. Joseph and Mary went to Bethlehem as they were descendants of King David and this was his birthplace. Upon arrival in Bethlehem, Mary gave birth to Jesus, God's Son. After the birth of the Christ Child there appeared a great star, which foretold the birth of a king. This star was sighted in the East by Wise Men, advisors to kings, and they recognized the star as a sign of the birth of a King of kings. They immediately made plans to travel to the west to find this king and pay homage and bring him gifts.

When Herod heard their story, he was furious with the thought that another king might take his place. He inquired of the scribes and teachers of the law to seek out where this child was to be born. Upon finding out that it was in Bethlehem, Herod told the Wise Men where to find this newborn king and then began to lay plans to destroy him.

The purpose and the hope of his coming is expressed in the scripture, "For God so loved the world that he gave his only Son, so that everyone who believes in him may not perish but may have eternal life" (John 3:16).

(Augustus stamps the scepter on the floor three times and bends it forward. His Advisor comes forward.)

Advisor: Yes, O honorable Lord, king of the entire universe, what do you wish?

Augustus: Hear this! Hear this! I do hereby decree this day ...

Advisor: *(bowing low)* Yes, your majesty.

Augustus: In order to have a complete record of all who will be taxed in my kingdom, I decree a census will be undertaken throughout the whole of the universe — my Roman Empire.

Advisor: Yes, sir. And how will this census be taken?

Augustus: Every man over the age of twelve must go to the town of his ancestor where he will register himself.

Advisor: Every man, sir?

Augustus: Every man ... by penalty of death!

(Drummer does a drum crash and roll.)

Advisor: *(bows low)* It shall be done, O great and wonderful lord.

(Lights dim. Augustus, Guard, and Advisor leave and walk to the back of the room. A red cloth is thrown over the throne chair.)

Children's Choir   "O Little Town Of Bethlehem"

Scene Two

(Spotlight goes to Joseph and Mary as they enter slowly down the center aisle. When they get to the front, they cross over to stage left. Joseph spreads a shawl over a small chair and helps Mary onto it. Mary takes a doll from hiding and holds it tenderly. Or a mother could bring a real baby up the aisle and give to Mary.)

Narrator: Joseph went from the town of Nazareth in Galilee to the town of Bethlehem in Judea for he was a descendant of King David. He went to register himself for the taxes with Mary, who was promised in marriage to him and was with child. While they were in Bethlehem, the time came for her to have her baby. She gave birth to her first son, wrapped him in swaddling clothes, and laid him in a manger for there was no room for them to stay in the inn.

Reader: In the beginning was the Word, and the Word was with God, and the Word was God. He was in the beginning with God. All things came into being through him, and without him not one thing came into being. What has come into being in him was life, and the life was the light of all people. The light shines in the darkness, and the darkness did not overcome it (John 1:1-5).

(Lights dim and then brighten to denote the passing of time.)

Narrator: Some men who studied the stars came from the East. At that time Herod was the king who sat upon the throne in Jerusalem. As the Wise Men entered the city with their great caravan, the people of the city were frightened, but curious and excited. The strangers asked for an audience before King Herod.

(While the Narrator is speaking, Three Wise Men in flowing robes enter right side and stride majestically down the aisle as the drum beats softly. Herod enters down center aisle and sits upon his throne. He looks a bit nervous and worried. His Guard stands on his left side, with spear in hand. The Three Wise Men stop at the foot of the stairs before Herod.)

Herod: *(loudly)* And, who are you?

First Wise Man: *(with dignity)* O Great King of Jerusalem and the land of Judah, we request an audience before you.

Herod: *(holds forth his scepter which is considerably smaller than the one Augustus had)* You may approach. Identify yourselves.

(Wise Men approach Herod's throne.)

Second Wise Man: We come from the East, beyond the great river.

Third Wise Man: We are advisors to kings in the East.

First Wise Man: We have studied the heavens, and in the stars we see a great and wonderful happening.

Herod: *(impatiently)* Yes, and what did you see?

Second Wise Man: A new star in the east. It was big and bright.

Third Wise Man: According to our study it tells of a ruler who shall be the King of all kings.

Herod: *(alarmed)* A king? But, but ... but, *I am the king* — the only king.

Third Wise Man: We have come to find the newborn child who is destined to become the King of the Jews. Where may we find him?

First Wise Man: We have come to worship him.

Herod: *(stomps feet, shakes with anger, then calms himself, and speaks condescendingly)* You have traveled far, you must be tired. Stay this night, so we may talk in the morning.

(The Three Wise Men leave Herod and move back down center aisle.)

Herod: *(shakes his scepter)* Ahaz! Ahaz, come here!

Ahaz: *(bows low)* Yes, O great Herod.

Herod: Call together all the chief priests! And, and the teachers of the law, too.

Ahaz: Yes, your majesty. *(backs away as he bows)*

(Ahaz stands center front and faces audience. He addresses the audience as if they were the people of Jerusalem.)

Ahaz: Hear ye, hear ye, all you people of Jerusalem. By order of the king, Herod the Great, all chief priests and teachers of the law are commanded to immediately appear before him.

(Lights dim and brighten to denote passing of time. Priests and Teachers are seated randomly throughout the audience.)

Scene Three

Herod: *(steps down from his throne and stands in the front of the audience)* You, chief priests and men of learning. *(begins to swagger and strut, holding the scepter high in front of him)* We have had visitors this day. They are learned men from the East, and advisors to kings. They tell of a star in the East which foretells the birth of another king. They say *(cringing)* that this child is to be the King of the Jews!

Priests and Teachers: *(gasps)* Ohhh!

(Drummer does a drum roll menacingly.)

Herod: *(sneering sarcastically)* What do *you* say, O wise and trusted men?

Priest One: Herod, oh great king. You are the only king of all Judea.

Priest Two: We do not follow any other king ...

Herod: *(interrupting)* Be still you pompous, sniveling dogs! I do not want to hear your lies.

(Priests are silent but squirm in their seats.)

(Drummer beats drum slowly.)

Herod: Speak, or every one of you will be thrown into prison.

(Loud crash of drum and then a single drum roll that tapers off to a sharp slow tap. Priests and Teachers are silent. A soft spotlight goes to the Nativity scene on the side.)

Teacher One: *(sitting near to the back, he stands, then holds a scroll before him/her — clears throat and speaks with difficulty)* King Herod *(clears his throat again)*, it is so written by our prophet Micah: "But you, O Bethlehem of Ephrathah, who are one of the little clans of Judah, from you shall come forth for me one who is to rule in Israel, whose origin is from of old, from ancient days" (Micah 5:2).

Herod: Bethlehem? But, Bethlehem is but an insignificant town. It cannot be important enough for a king to be born there.

Teacher Two: *(with dignity)* And he shall stand and feed his flock in the strength of the Lord, in the majesty of the name of the Lord his God (Micah 5:4a).

Herod: *(surprised)* Bethlehem?

Teacher Three: *(proudly)* And they shall live secure, for now he shall be great to the ends of the earth; and he shall be the one of peace (Micah 5:4b-5).

(Herod is stunned, shocked, and silent. Then shaking with anger he raises his scepter and shakes it menacingly. The Priests and Teachers sit down.)

Herod: *(loudly)* You vile traitors! Get out. Get out of here! *(stalks back to his throne where he sits quietly and ponders his situation)* Ahaz! Ahaz! Bring those pompous, know-it-all pigs to me immediately.

(Ahaz goes to get the Three Wise Men. He brings them before Herod. The Wise Men enter with great dignity and bow before the king.)

Herod: Ahaz, Guard, remove yourselves. *(waves his hand at guard)* Go away.

(Ahaz and Guard leave by center aisle.)

Herod: *(smirking)* You! *(pointing at the Wise Men)* You men from the East, come before me.

First Wise Man: *(moving forward)* O yes, great king of Judah.

Herod: Tell me. Just when did you first see this star that foretells this birth?

Second Wise Man: We began our journey one moon after we first saw the star.

Third Wise Man: We have been traveling for seven moons.

Herod: Ahhhhh! *(ponders for a time)* Go. Go toward Bethlehem and make a careful search for the child.

First Wise Man: Bethlehem, the city of David?

Herod: Yes, and when you find him *(smiles to himself)*, return to Jerusalem and let me know where he is *(touches finger to side of nose)* so that I, too, may go *(cough, cough)* — that I, too, may go and worship him.

Scene Four

(The Wise Men turn and walk slowly toward Bethlehem. They leave by way of the center aisle and walk toward the back of the sanctuary. Drummer beats steady, slow rhythm throughout the march down the center aisle to the back.)

Choir   "Wise Men Follow Jesus" or "We Three Kings"

(As the choir sings, the Three Wise Men enter up left aisle and go to the manger. They bow before the baby and set their gifts before him. After Narrator has finished, the Three Wise Men turn and leave down the right aisle.)

Narrator: And when they saw the child with his mother, Mary, they knelt and worshiped him. They brought out their gifts of gold, frankincense, and myrrh and presented them to him. They then returned to their country by another route since God and warned them in a dream not to go back to Herod.

Narrator: After they had left, an angel of the Lord appeared to Joseph in a dream.

Angel One: Joseph! Herod will be looking for the child in order to kill him. Get up and take the child and his mother and go to the land of Egypt. Stay there until I tell you to return.

(Joseph puts a shawl around Mary's shoulders as she stands with baby. Joseph then picks up their bedroll and leaves the same way the Wise Men left. Lights dim. Drum beats slowly as they start to leave ... slowly and softly and sadly. Joseph and Mary walk to the beat of the drum.)

Angel One: In the beginning was the Word, and the Word was with God, and the Word was God. He was in the beginning with God. All things came into being through him, and without him not one thing came into being. What has come into being in him was life, and the life was the light of all people. The light shines in the darkness, and the darkness did not overcome it (John 1:1-5).

Angel Two: For God so loved the world that he gave his only Son, so that everyone who believes in him may not perish but may have eternal life (John 3:16).

The End

Where Is Your Lamb?

I am the good shepherd. I know my own and my own know me, just as the Father knows me and I know the Father. And I lay down my life for the sheep. I have other sheep that do not belong to this fold. I must bring them also, and they will listen to my voice. So there will be one flock, one shepherd.
— John 10:14-17

Characters

Storyteller	Silas
Cantor	Daniel
Mary	Sarah
Angel	Ruth
Choir	Joab
Eli	Joseph
Lydia	

Scene One

(The Storyteller stands at a podium or is seated on a comfortable chair, at left stage. The Cantor, Mary, and Angel stand at the far right side of the audience.)

Choir   "O Come, O Come, Emmanuel"

Storyteller: Come and celebrate the story of the birth of Jesus, the Son of God. This Jesus was called to "preach the good news to the poor."

Cantor: For he is our God, and we are the people of his pasture, and the sheep of his hand (Psalm 95:7).

Storyteller: *(opens large book on lap)* Many years ago in Galilee, in a town named Nazareth, during the time when Herod was King of Judea, there lived a carpenter named Joseph. He was proud of the fact that he could trace his ancestry back to King David, and he took special care to worship God and obey his commands. Even though he was a young man, he was already accomplished at his trade and was sought out to make tools and furniture by the people of his town. As Joseph smoothed the rough edges of a chest he was working on, he thought of his good fortune. His business had increased, and he was looked on with favor as an excellent carpenter. He looked forward to the coming spring when his childhood friend, lovely Mary, would be his bride. He had been working hard and soon their home would be ready. Even under the oppression of their Roman rulers, his life looked promising indeed.

Cantor: Then we your people, the flock of your pasture, will give thanks to you forever; from generation to generation we will recount your praise (Psalm 79:13).

Storyteller: Mary was very young and was promised in marriage for several years to Joseph, a descendant of King David. The time was coming soon when she would leave the comfort of her family home and move into the new home that Joseph had been busy preparing for their life together. Theirs was going to be a special union because they were truly fond of one another, and she, too, was a descendant of King David.

51

Cantor: Know that the Lord is God. It is he that made us, and we are his; we are his people, and the sheep of his pasture (Psalms 100:3).

Storyteller: That evening as Mary said her evening prayers, the Angel Gabriel appeared to her. Gabriel was sent by God with a very special message for her.

Angel: Greetings, favored one! The Lord is with you. Do not be afraid, Mary, for you have found favor with God. And now, you will conceive in your womb and bear a son, and you will name him Jesus. He will be great, and will be called the Son of the Most High, and the Lord God will give to him the throne of his ancestor David. He will reign over the house of Jacob forever, and of his kingdom there will be no end (Luke 1:28b, 30b-33).

Mary: My soul magnifies the Lord, and my spirit rejoices in God my Savior, for he has looked with favor on the lowliness of his servant. Surely, from now on all generations will call me blessed; for the Mighty One has done great things for me, and holy is his name (Luke 1:47-49).

Choir   "Lo, How A Rose E'er Blooming"

Storyteller: Joseph was a man who always did what was right, but when he found that Mary was pregnant he despaired. He loved Mary a great deal and did not want to disgrace her, but he decided that he would break the engagement privately. That night, as he slept, an angel of the Lord appeared to him in a dream.

Angel: Joseph, son of David, do not be afraid to take Mary as your wife, for the child conceived in her is from the Holy Spirit. She will bear a son, and you are to name him Jesus, for he will save his people from their sins (Matthew 1:20b-21).

Cantor: All this took place to fulfill what had been spoken by the Lord through the prophet: "Look, the virgin shall conceive and bear a son, and they shall name him Emmanuel, which means 'God is with us'" (Matthew 1:22-23).

Storyteller: When Joseph awoke from sleep, he did as the angel of the Lord commanded him; he took her as his wife, but had no marital relations with her until she had borne a son, and he named him Jesus (Matthew 1:24-25).

Scene Two

(It is morning in the Bethlehem home of a family of shepherds. There are several children sleeping on the floor on sleeping mats. Lydia enters and goes about the task of making bread on a table. She hums quietly to herself.)

Eli: *(sits up and rubs eyes)* It's cold in here.

Lydia: Good morning, Eli. Yes, it is damp and cold. Please bring in some dry wood and build a fire. The bread will be ready for the oven soon.

(Eli groans and yawns but gets up, rolls bedroll, and goes outside.)

Silas: *(looking out through the doorway from his bed)* Is it morning already? Hey, it's raining out and we have to take the sheep out to pasture today.

(Daniel rolls over and pulls blankets over head.)

Lydia: Come now, Daniel. It's time to roll up your bedroll.

(Daniel pulls blankets up tighter and rolls himself into a ball.)

Sarah: *(crawls out of bedroll, rolls it up, and stacks it in corner of the room)* Good morning, Mother.

Ruth: *(awakens, and sits up)* I was having the strangest dream. There were angels looking at us and ... and they were singing.

Lydia: Angels? That sounds like a nice dream. I wonder what that could mean?

Ruth: It was such a happy dream, I want to just stay here and go back to sleep.

Joab: *(enters from side room)* Get up, my children. We have a busy day today.

Eli: *(enters carrying wood which he places in the oven and lights the fire)* Yes, Father. We have to take the sheep out on the hillside. With all this rain the grass should be fresh and green.

Joab: The rains came just in time for the farmers to plant the hay.

Silas: This rain will make the trip difficult with all the water rushing down the hillsides.

Joab: Yes, the going will be hard on everyone. I'm not sure Daniel should go with us this time. It may be too dangerous.

Daniel: *(peeks out of bedroll holding a stuffed lamb)* But you promised, Father. You can't take Tabitha out on the hillside without me.

Joab: Mother and I will have to talk about it, Daniel.

Daniel: *(rolls out of bedroll, bundles it up in a heap, and throws it in the corner; Sarah goes over and rolls it neatly to stack with the others)* But you promised, Father! I'll do everything you ask me to, I promise.

Silas: *(getting out of bed and rolling his bedroll for carrying)* Then it looks like we need to get an early start. I'm hungry. Is the bread ready?

Lydia: The oven's just getting hot enough to start the cooking. Sarah, run down to the well and bring us fresh water. Ruth, bring in the figs and cheese.

Joab: I've seen to the sheep, they are ready to travel. Now Eli, see that our warm clothes are wrapped securely against the rain. Silas, prepare the bedrolls and then help me get the food ready to carry.

(All go about their tasks, then come to the table one by one.)

Joab: *(bows head and prays)* O Lord, our God. Your greatness is seen in all the world! We thank you for our home and family and the food before us. We come to you for protection as we begin our journey into the fields, for you alone keep us safe. Shalom.

(They eat and chat quietly.)

Joab: What do you think, Lydia? Is Daniel ready to spend a few nights out in the fields?

Lydia: The weather is bad and he is very young ... but he needs to learn.

Eli: I was younger than Daniel when I first went with Father into the fields.

Lydia: But this weather is so unpredictable, I can't help but worry.

Joab: He is really not too young, and he cares about his pet lamb; that should help. I'll watch him carefully.

Lydia: Very well, the rain can't last too long, and I know that you will watch him closely.

(When they are through, Silas carefully wraps the leftover cheese and figs to carry on their journey. Father bundles his clothes and throws them over his shoulder. Eli and Silas do the same. Daniel picks up his lamb and puts his bedroll over his shoulder. They head out the door.)

Joab: *(to Lydia)* We plan to head north, you should see us in about a week.

Lydia: Take care my brave, young men. Our prayers go with you.

(The Shepherds leave with sheep at their side [small children wearing white clothing and sheep ears]. They walk slowly to the back of the room and stop to chat from time to time. When they leave, the house area is reset for the Nativity scene with a small chair and manger.)

Cantor: The Lord is my shepherd; I shall not want (Psalm 23:1).

(The Shepherds go to the back left corner of the room. They can be heard but not seen by the congregation.)

Daniel: Father, are we almost there?

Joab: Watch closely, my sons, this area is very dangerous. The ledge is narrow, and you must stay close to the sides of the cliffs.

Silas: I've gathered as many lambs as I can handle, I'll lead the way.

Eli: The rain has made the path very slippery.

Daniel: O Father, I'm scared.

Joab: Here, Daniel, take my hand and stay close to the wall.

Cantor: Even though I walk through the darkest valley, I fear no evil; for you are with me; your rod and your staff — they comfort me (Psalm 23:4).

Silas: We are past the hardest part now; it looks as if we all made it safely, and all the sheep are accounted for.

Daniel: Father, are we almost there?

Eli: This looks like a good place to camp, Father. The grass is green, and we are all tired from our climb through the canyon.

Joab: The water is running too fast for the sheep. We must go on.

(The Shepherds walk to a spot at the left side, where they can be seen by the congregation. Here they sit down.)

Silas: This looks like a good place, and I can go no further!

Joab: Yes, the pasture is good and there is a quiet stream close by. We'll settle here.

Cantor: He makes me lie down in green pastures; he leads me beside still waters; he restores my soul. He leads me in right paths for his name's sake (Psalm 23:2-3).

(The Shepherds spread out their bedrolls on the green grass. Each takes out some cheese and starts to eat as the Choir sings.)

Choir   "The Lord's My Shepherd"

Storyteller: The one who enters by the gate is the shepherd of the sheep. The gatekeeper opens the gate for him, and the sheep hear his voice. He calls his own sheep by name and leads them out. When he has brought out all his own, he goes ahead of them, and the sheep follow him because they know his voice. They will not follow a stranger, but they will run from him because they do not know the voice of strangers (John 10:2-5).

Cantor: Very truly, I tell you, I am the gate for the sheep. All who came before me are thieves and bandits; but the sheep did not listen to them. I am the gate. Whoever enters by me will be saved, and will come in and go out and find pasture. The thief comes only to steal and kill and destroy. I came that they may have life, and have it abundantly (John 10:7b-10).

(Daniel sets his lamb on the ground next to him and begins to eat his cheese. A string has been attached to Daniel's stuffed lamb. While Daniel is preoccupied with eating and humming to himself, the lamb is slowly pulled away from him and hidden from sight.)

Daniel: *(looks around)* Tabitha ... Tabitha, where are you? Tabitha? Tabitha?

Eli: What's wrong, Daniel? What's the matter?

Daniel: Tabitha was right next to me. Now she's gone. Did you see where she went?

Silas: You've lost Tabitha already? We just got here. Oh well, I'll help you look.

(Everyone looks for Tabitha. They look everywhere around the area until, finally, they return shaking their heads.)

Daniel: Oh, Father, Tabitha is lost. What can I do?

(Lights dim.)

Joab: There is nothing we can do. It is getting dark and we have looked everywhere.

(Daniel sits close to his father and wipes his eyes.)

Choir   "Father, Loving Father" (vv. 1-3) by Jean Milane Gower

Cantor: All we like sheep have gone astray; we have all turned to our own way, and the Lord has laid on him the iniquity of us all (Isaiah 53:6).

Storyteller: As our shepherds sleep an uneasy sleep, a new drama unfolds. At that time Emperor Augustus, had ordered a census to be taken throughout the Roman Empire. Everyone, then, went to register himself, each to his own hometown.

Cantor: And you, Bethlehem in the land of Judah, are by no means least among the rulers of Judah; for from you shall come a ruler who is to shepherd my people Israel (Matthew 2:6). *(pauses)* Joseph also went from the town of Nazareth in Galilee to Judea, to the city of David called Bethlehem, because he was descended from the house and family of David. He went to be registered with Mary, to whom he was engaged and who was expecting a child (Luke 2:4-5).

(Mary and Joseph enter right side aisle.)

Storyteller: Early the next morning we see a young couple making their weary way along the rugged road.

Mary: Oh, Joseph, I fear the child is due very soon. We need to find shelter.

Joseph: I know you're tired, Mary, but it won't be long now. Bethlehem is just a few miles up this road.

(A soft baaaaa is heard from backstage. Mary and Joseph stop and look up. There on a ledge they see Tabitha, the lamb.)

Joseph: Well, what do we have here? You poor, little lamb you are all alone. You must be lost. Here, come let me help you.

(Joseph lifts the lamb off the ledge and cradles it in his arms.)

Mary: *(hands shawl to Joseph with which he wraps the lamb)* Why the poor thing is shaking with cold and fear. Here, wrap it up in my shawl.

Joseph: Little lost lamb, let us look for your shepherd.

(Joseph and Mary continue on pathway until they come across the Shepherds who are just awakening.)

Joseph: Greetings, my friends. We found this frightened little lamb out on a big rock. Does it belong to you?

Silas: Greetings, strangers. Yes, yes, that is Tabitha. She wandered off last night, and my younger brother, Daniel, has been beside himself ever since.

Daniel: *(running up to Joseph and taking his lamb, he cuddles it tightly)* Tabitha, Tabitha ... my little Tabitha.

Joab: We want to thank you, strangers. We were worried about this little one. We are grateful that you have returned her to us. Please sit down and share our bread with us.

Joseph: Thank you. We are hungry. We have been hurrying to get to Bethlehem. Mary feels that the child is coming soon, and we need to find shelter.

(Joseph and Mary sit down and eat.)

Silas: Are you of the family of Jesse? We have seen many of his people coming into town to register for the taxes.

Joseph: Yes. Both Mary and myself are descendants of King David and are here to register ourselves as commanded by the emperor.

Eli: It really makes me angry that we are under the thumbs of those Romans. We are poor shepherds, and now we will have to pay more taxes to those ... those ...

Joab: Take care of how you speak of those who rule over us, Eli. It is not safe to speak of how you feel.

Silas: *(after awkward silence)* It has been good talking with you strangers, but we do need to watch over the sheep.

Joseph: Then we had best be on our way. Thank you for sharing your meal with us. Come, Mary, it isn't much farther.

(Joseph and Mary move on toward Bethlehem. The Nativity scene is set in the area where the Shepherds' house had been, and Joseph and Mary take their places. Mary picks up baby and holds it.)

Storyteller: And while they were in Bethlehem, the time came for her to have her baby. She gave birth to her first son, wrapped him in swaddling cloths and laid him in a manger as there was no room for them to stay in the inn.

(The Shepherds settle down with their sheep. The lights dim.)

Storyteller: While the shepherds settled in for the night, an Angel of the Lord appeared to them, and the glory of the Lord shone over them.

Angel: Do not be afraid; for see — I am bringing you good news of great joy for all the people: to you is born this day in the city of David a Savior, who is the Messiah, the Lord. This will be a sign for you: you will find a child wrapped in bands of cloth and lying in a manger (Luke 2:10b-12).

Storyteller: Suddenly an army of heaven's angels appeared with angels singing praises to God:

Choir   "Hark! The Herald Angels Sing"

Storyteller: When the angels went away from them back into heaven, all was quiet once more.

Joab: Let us go into Bethlehem and see this thing which the Lord has said.

(Shepherds gather their sheep and head for Bethlehem. They need to return the way they came. As they enter the far side of town, they meet Lydia returning from the well with a jug of water on her shoulder.)

Lydia: Joab? My sons? What are you doing back in town?

Joab: Lydia, the most amazing thing just happened! As we were sleeping on the hillside with our sheep we were surrounded by angels. Yes, angels.

Eli: And they praised God and sang to us.

Silas: They told of us that a baby, the Messiah, was born last night right here in Bethlehem.

Joab: They said that he was Christ the Lord! And that we would find him wrapped in swaddling cloths and lying in a manger.

Daniel: *(pointing)* Father, there's the stable; there's a manger in there.

Joab: It is strange that the Messiah would be born in a stable, but let's go look.

(The Shepherd family enters the stable.)

Storyteller: So they hurried off and found Mary and Joseph and saw the baby lying in the manger. When the shepherds saw him, they told them what the angel had said about the child. All who heard it were amazed at what the shepherds said.

Choir   "Away In A Manger"

Cantor: But Mary remembered all these words and pondered them in her heart (Luke 2:19).

Lydia: *(leaves stable and calls out as she runs to other side of stage)* I must run and tell my daughters.

Lydia: *(calling as she runs)* Girls, girls ... light a torch and come quickly to the stable! The most wonderful thing has happened!

Choir   "Bring A Torch, Jeanette, Isabella"

(As Choir sings, the daughters return to the stable with a torch and greet Mary, Joseph, and the baby in the manger.)

The End

CPSIA information can be obtained at www.ICGtesting.com
Printed in the USA
LVOW09s1121270815

451776LV00005B/159/P